Copyright © 2023 by Cyril & Dorise Publishing

All rights reserved.

No part of this publication may be reproduced, distributed, or transmitted in any
form or by any means, including photocopying, recording, or other electronic or
mechanical methods, without the prior written permission of the publisher,
except in the case of brief quotations embodied in critical reviews and certain
other non-commercial uses permitted by copyright law.

For permission requests, write to the publisher, addressed "Attention:
Permissions Coordinator," at the address below.

Harmony Close,
Kewtown,
Providenciales
Turks & Caicos Islands

ISBN: 9781739369149

https://www.cyrilanddorsiepublishing.com/

GOD WILL MAKE YOU LAUGH

TABLE OF CONTENTS

I	Don't Let The Enemy SIlence You	1
II	Get Up	6
III	Never Say Never	8
IV	Stay Positive	14
V	There Is No Fear In Love	18
VI	The Road To Healing	21
VII	My Mess, His Messenger	26

God Will Make You Laugh

Holy Spirit,
I pray for the individuals
reading this book to be blessed
and that their understanding is
enlightened, hope restored, and every
feeling of illusion be put to shame
through the blood of Jesus.

Amen.

CHAPTER 1
Don't Let The Enemy Silence You

Chapter One
Don't Let The Enemy Silence You

Today, I want you to walk with me as we seek the truth from God's Word.

Many of you may wonder, is my present situation my permanent place? I remember being a prisoner in my mind for many years; life's doubt, fear, and anxiety had left me a broken soldier along life's path. These are the situations the enemy uses to discourage you from getting up; his main goal is to cripple you so that you can never get up to fulfill the purpose that our Lord and Saviour Jesus Christ has called you to. If you want to change your situation, you must first be willing to identify the many tools the enemy uses to bind you. The enemy knows you are under the influence of a mind attack because he did it in the first place.

> ***For we wrestle not against flesh and blood, but against principalities, against powers, against the rulers of the darkness of this world, against spiritual wickedness in high places.***
>
> **Ephesians 6:12**

The enemy is well-equipped to fight you in any way possible. He knows our fight is not with each other. So often, I had this fight. He was at work in my mind. I am addressing this because it has crippled many of us, believing human beings are our fight. I had to learn that even though it seemed like my sisters and brothers were fighting me, it was the strong man behind it that I could not see. The enemy is much aware, and his job is to wreak havoc in our lives so that we can stay in our current situations, especially when he knows God has more in store for us.

No man can enter into a strong man's house, and spoil his goods, except he will first bind the strong man; and then he will spoil his house.
Mark 3:27

The enemy knows that you're the best candidate to be preyed upon if you are unaware of your surroundings.

Remember, I told you earlier I had been a prisoner in my mind for many years, and my dreams had been shattered. Because of this stronghold, the enemy used his voice to speak defeat into me. His main goal was to frustrate me so that discouragement could set in.

Especially when he knows there are many open doors you are unaware of and do not know how to close.

As long as we are blind and unaware, we have been placed in a situation to be captivated by this enemy, Satan.

> **And the great dragon was cast out, that old serpent, called the Devil, and Satan, which deceiveth the whole world: he was cast out into the earth, and his angels were cast out with him.**
> **Revelation 12:9**

Satan knows he cannot enter the house of a strong man, except he first binds the strong man. We must be willing and ready to receive the Word of God and close every door so that there is no entry for him, especially if we will live successful lives.

I could recall many years ago how I was held a prisoner of fear, hopelessness, anxiety, and discouragement; these were areas of my life that I struggled with. It was other areas of life, but mainly the ones I mentioned. It was enough to abort any mission that God was leading me to. The enemy knew my weaknesses, and he was aware that I was a paralytic in these conditions; he made sure hope would be lost and that I would never be able to get up again.

4 If we say, We will enter into the city, then the famine is in the city, and we shall die there: and if we sit still here, we die also. Now therefore come, and let us fall unto the host of the Syrians: if they save us alive, we shall live; and if they kill us, we shall but die.

5 And they rose up in the twilight, to go unto the camp of the Syrians: and when they were come to the uttermost part of the camp of Syria, behold, there was no man there.

2 Kings 7:4-5

CHAPTER 2
Get Up

Chapter Two
Get Up

We must be able to get up and fight back if we will be victorious. God has a plan for all of us, and we must never say never if we will succeed.

Maybe you, like me, have lost hope, but we must be like the Syrians who were willing to get up and move toward the enemy camp, and if we perish, we perish. We must confront what is stopping us from coming into the will of God for our lives. The enemy's job is to frustrate us; once we become frustrated, we lose hope. God plans that we do not allow the prisoner of fear to cheat us out of his blessings. The devil hates to see us become strong. He knows that we will realize our strengths if we discover our weaknesses. Like me, you may face many of these struggles and feel like life has thrown a ball at you. It would be best if you never gave in to the many lies of the adversary. You must be determined to let go and let God. He wants you to be free, but you must first be willing to bind the strong man in the mind. In my next book, I will discuss this topic more, helping you understand that the battle is either won or lost in the mind. It's up to you, my friends, to let the healing begin. Once you have a made-up mind, there is no telling what God won't do.

CHAPTER 3

Never Say Never

Chapter Three
Never Say Never

Romans 4:17
(As it is written, I have made thee a father of many nations,) before him whom he believed, even God, who quickeneth the dead, and calleth those things which be not as though they were.

It would have seemed impossible if anyone had told me years ago that I would become an author. I remember finishing high school with a High School Certificate and a distinction in Biology. I had barely reached the finish line. Not only that, but I remember crying because I could not go to college; things were hard for my Mom, who was raising more than me. She didn't have it, and I could not obtain a government scholarship then. Like many of you, you may have passed through that same route and, like me, had become emotionally wrecked and ready to give up, feeling all hope is gone, as written in my previous book, *The Pain Was For My Gain*.

You would have realized that this has felt like a cage; when you are disappointed, angry, and frustrated, it opens the door for the enemy to enter. The voice of the enemy seems to be speaking louder than God. This was precisely what the enemy was doing. He aimed to stop the plan and purpose God had for me.

Like me, you probably wondered why you did not have a chance to succeed. Why were Jane, Mary, and Sue able to accomplish their mission? My friends, God never makes mistakes; His intentions toward us never fail. He wants us to reach our full potential, even when it seems like all hope is lost.

Jeremiah 29:11
For I know the thoughts that I think toward you, saith the Lord, thoughts of peace, and not of evil, to give you an expected end.

God has a perfect plan for all of us, and I realize He also has one for me. You, too, are on His mind. He knows what is best for you.

4 If we say, We will enter into the city, then the famine is in the city, and we shall die there: and if we sit still here, we die also. Now therefore come, and let us fall unto the host of the Syrians: if they save us alive, we shall live; and if they kill us, we shall but die.

5 And they rose up in the twilight, to go unto the camp of the Syrians: and when they were come to the uttermost part of the camp of Syria, behold, there was no man there.
2 Kings 7:4-5

My friends, God has a way of putting His children to the test. He knows our location, name, and address. He planned our future long before birth and knew the road we would take. Nothing ever takes God by surprise, and you were never a mistake. Even though the enemy makes us feel like a failure, God always proves the enemy wrong.

Before I formed thee, I knew thee and before thou camest forth out of the womb, I sanctified thee, and ordained thee a prophet unto the nation.
Jeremiah 1:5

I came to understand that God is all-knowing. He was concerned about me and determined that if I stayed with Him and obeyed His voice, I wouldn't be disappointed. I am here to tell you that God never gives up on us. We simply don't believe He can do it most of the time!

If you believe and have faith in others but find it very hard to think for yourself, this becomes a reality when you feel that only a particular class or group of individuals can succeed.

Friends, this is another lie the enemy has spoken into your ears.

I can do all things through Christ, which strengthens me.
Philippians 4:13

God wants us to be successful, but we must be willing to go all the way with Him. I didn't understand initially that it was after the rain that the sunshine would appear. Faithfulness to God is the key to success. Above everything else, His perfect will is that we come to our full potential in Him.

Beloved, I wish above all things that thou mayest prosper and be in health, even as the soul prospereth.
3 John 2:2

I couldn't understand that, at some point, above everything, God wished for me to live a healthy and prosperous life. Like many of you, my question was, why am I failing?

Why was I always sick? This was hard to comprehend. Friends, I realized I had to be processed, which was difficult.

To be truthful, when the enemy controls your mind, he puts you in such division that you're not even thinking straight.

Our minds must be in God, and His angels will guide them or we will be at a loss to Satan.

CHAPTER 4

Stay Positive

Chapter Four
Stay Positive

Let this mind be in you, which was also in Christ Jesus:
Philippians 2:5

Our minds are the battlegrounds; we must allow positive thoughts to enter them. I was letting the enemy speak defeat. He was constantly reminding me that I was an embarrassment and a failure. He told me I could never amount to anything and who would listen to me when I could hardly dot my Is and cross my Ts. I often gave in to him, failing to say what God wanted me to say. Note that the enemy plans to keep you silent. He uses his weapons so that you don't glorify God. After attending evening service, I remember multiple times when the enemy would tell me, "Don't ever testify." If you are like me, I loved the church; I just wanted to be there, even if I was not a part of anything. I recall a night many years ago when the Spirit of God came upon me. I wanted to testify, but the enemy sat precisely where I was and whispered again. He said, "Don't make a fool out of yourself." These people will laugh you to scorn. Friends, the enemy, will never stop. It is his job to ensure you don't get to where God wants you to be, and I also realize that I had to develop the courage that only God could give me.

***Let your light so shine before men,
that they may see your good works, and glorify your Father
which is in heaven.
Matthew 5:16***

Friends, if we are going to be victorious, we must be willing to be the lighthouses that God calls us to be. Remember I told you earlier that fear started to get a hold of me? One of the tools that the enemy uses to cripple our ministry, goals, or whatever God has in store for us is fear. Fear brings torment.

I remember many times along life's path when this enemy called fear hit me. It had somewhat crippled me, so I didn't want to see the sunlight. I stayed inside instead. I am addressing this enemy because fear within itself is a mighty stronghold; many of our dreams and aspirations have stopped. Furthermore, I had struggled with it, but God is a strong deliverer, and he had allowed me to break free from this chain so that I could come forth.

***And that they may recover themselves
out of the snare of the devil, who are
taken captive by him at his will. 2 Timothy 2:26***

God has called us out of the trap, and we must be willing to break free of this stronghold that is fear. If we go to the next dimension of our lives, we must be willing to put God first and love Him with all our hearts. So often, we say we love God, but our action shows otherwise by being contrary to His will. Many times in my walk with God, I became confused. My spiritual eyes were closed. The enemy wanted me to see something different. I was still fearing him when it was God that I should have continually been fearing.

The enemy doesn't care if you are attending church, singing in the choir, or even praying aloud as long as your actions towards God are not genuine; he loves when we play church. I had to learn this, and I am also doing my best to help you understand. There must be a sincere love for God, and your worship must be genuine. God is perfect in all His ways. When we become perfect, then perfect love will cast out our fears.

CHAPTER 5
There Is No Fear In Love

Chapter Five
There Is No Fear in Love

There is no fear in love; but perfect love casteth out fear: because fear hath torment. He that feareth is not made perfect in love.

1John 4:18

My friends, I know what you are thinking. Like me, I was also confused until I finally understood that God was telling me to grow up, in other words, to get mature. If you are not maturing in the things of God by loving Him with all your heart, you're a candidate for the enemy called fear.

Be ye therefore perfect, even as your Father which is in heaven is perfect.

Matthew 5:48

Our Father is mature in all His ways, and as His children, He desires us to be as mature or perfect as He is. Even though we are not equal to God, He expects us as His children to take responsibility by loving Him enough so that the enemy won't be able to cast us down with fear. When we exercise maturity, no demon on planet Earth can silence us when we express or have a genuine love for God.

The wicked flee when no man pursueth: but the righteous are bold as a lion.
Proverbs 28:1

Instead of the enemy sitting, pursuing me, I am now chasing him away. Even the devil is aware when the anointing of God is at work in our lives. God has given us power over the forces of darkness, and the greater one lives within us. We must never be afraid to testify of the goodness of God.

CHAPTER 6

The Road to Healing

Chapter Six
The Road To Healing

We must be willing to be healed from the wounds of our past despite the many scars; it should be a reminder that God's goodness kept us functioning in our rightful minds. We must always acknowledge that it is God who brings us by way of crisis and that He predestined our lives. Furthermore, we must begin to speak those thoughts into existence.

But the Lord said unto me, Say not, I am a child: for thou shal go to all that I shall send thee, and whatsoever I command thee thou shalt speak.
Jeremiah 1:7

Like the prophet Jeremiah, I, too, had not one but many excuses. Maybe you're reading this and may have asked God many questions about why you've been in a stagnated place for so long, with shattered dreams. But we must be willing to go wherever God wants us to and know that even though every situation looks impossible, they are possible when God is in it.

It took me some time to comprehend that God does understand and that everything has a time and a season, but we must be willing to embrace our change when it comes. We must be willing to stand up amid adversity, even when the enemy's voice seems louder. God promises to go with us each step of the way, and all He wants from us is a yes!

For the Lord God is a sun and shield: the Lord will give grace and glory: no good thing will he withhold from them that walk uprightly.

Psalms 84:11

God's promises are sure. He wants you to overcome every obstacle holding you captive; like me, you may have wondered, will I ever get that job, raise a family, or write my story? The answer is yes, but you must be willing to let the Lord take complete control of every situation you face. God has a set time for us all. He will make you laugh; His favor is sure; you must not faint!

Thou shalt arise, and have mercy upon Zion: for the time to favour her, yea, the set time, is come.
Psalms 102:13

Many times in my life, I have experienced multiple delays. Some I see as intentional, others I thought of as my fault, but ultimately, I realize God doesn't see as man see. His delays are always for our good. We must be confident even when we don't understand, and if I'm honest, the end product always proves excellent because, most times, God stops us from danger ahead. He allows the enemies to pass by before us, so by the time we arrive, he's off the scene.

We must see the bigger picture; God will not allow us to die prematurely in the wilderness. His plans and purposes for our life will speak volumes when He's finished. It will amaze your adversaries, but you must never give in to the noises of the enemy. It's his way of stopping you from reaching your heights, depths, and measures.

And this word, Yet once more, signifieth the removing of those things that are shaken, as of things that are made, that those things which cannot be shaken may remain. Hebrews 12:27

We must become strong roots of hope and courage and see each job done in the spirit and the natural. Like the prophet Jeremiah, you must accept God's command. You have been given a mandate throughout the challenge that God is walking with you.

He is the one who is speaking through you. His presence is your protection. He promises to keep you through every sphere of life.

I have learned that despite my disabilities, I never gave up. I worked with what I had, kindly took a leap of faith, and ran with it. It was not easy initially to deal with rejection, low self-esteem, and criticism. But I recognize that in all of this, the enemy was at his best for me to fail. I am writing this book because I am convinced that, like myself, many still believe and confess the lies that the enemy is telling them, but you must be able to reject his many lies. You are an overcomer and will survive every storm he throws at you. By faith, I can see you at the finish line.
Today, I declare that God has tremendously blessed me in all areas of my life. There is no telling what God won't do for us when we take that leap of faith.

But the anointing which ye have received of him abideth in you, and ye need not that any man teach you: but as the same anointing teacheth you of all things, and is truth, and is no lie, and even as it hath taught you, ye shall abide in him.
1John 2:27

CHAPTER 7

My Mess, His Messenger

Chapter Seven
My Mess, His Messenger

God is willing to take your mess and make it into a message, but you must complete the many challenges you thought you could not. No matter how painful the price, you must be willing to raise your banner above that of the enemy. To do so, your mindset must change, and faith must be your main priority here. You cannot afford to lose hope now. Your failures are turning into triumphs; no wonder the enemy has held you captive in your mind for so long; he knows now that your eyes are open, there is no telling how quickly you will soar above your prey. God has a way of making you and me laugh after all the enemy has done to us. God is determined that the enemy won't triumph over us; His plan for you is that we come to His expected end. After all, what seems impossible with man is possible with God. He knows our name and address, and He has always been aware of our struggles. Even in our darkest night, He was there.

The truth is, my friends, He wanted us to acknowledge that it is only through Him that we live and have our being.

No matter the situation, His anointing makes the difference. I am a testament to His truth; His Holy Spirit became my teacher. Today, I am bringing hope and restoration where many have lost it. May you gladly receive your Ph.D. through the Holy Spirit, calling darkness into light. The Lord will make you laugh.

Revelation 22:17

And the Spirit and the bride say, Come. And let him that heareth say, Come. And let him that is athirst come. And whosoever will, let him take the water of life freely.

ABOUT
THE AUTHOR

Apostle Rosemary Duncanson is a unique and rare vessel to the body of Christ. Apostle Duncanson was born in the Turks and Caicos Islands; she is a mother, Pastor, and Teacher. Having proclaimed the Word of God for more than three decades, her yoke-breaking anointing has helped many across all spheres of life. Apostle Dunacanson enjoys her outreach ministries and reaches out to as many as possible, calling darkness into light. After many years of pain, hurt, and disappointments, she is proving her ministries entirely and is determined that the enemy will not win. Her determination has given her recognition in every area of her life.

Letters To God

Letters To God

Letters To God

Letters To God

Letters To God

Letters To God

Letters To God

www.ingramcontent.com/pod-product-compliance
Lightning Source LLC
Chambersburg PA
CBHW061147170426
43209CB00011B/1585